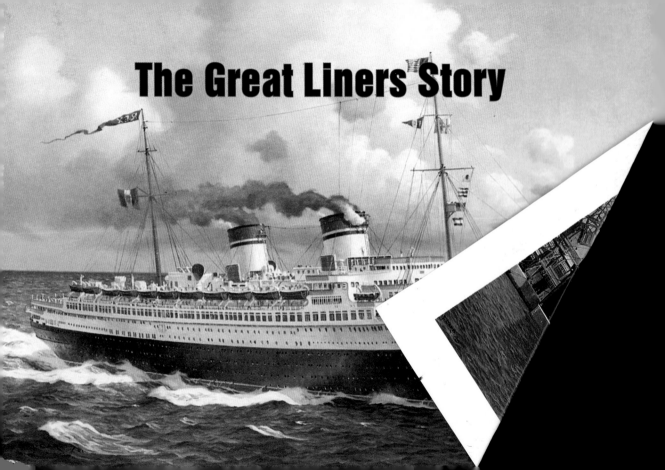

# The Great Liners Story

# The Great Liners Story

## William H. Miller

The History Press

Published in the United Kingdom in 2012 by
The History Press
The Mill · Brimscombe Port · Stroud · Gloucestershire · GL5 2QG

British Library Cataloguing in Publication Data
A catalogue record for this book is available from the British
Library.

Hardback ISBN 978-0-7524-6452-7

Typesetting and origination by The History Press
Manufacturing managed by Jellyfish Print Solutions Ltd
Printed in India

Half title page: *The glorious* Rex *underway,
preparing for an arrival at New York, in a superb
painting by Stephen Card. (Stephen Card Collection)*

Half title verso: *In another very fine painting
by Stephen Card, the world's largest liner, the*
Queen Elizabeth, *is seen at the Ocean Terminal
at Southampton. These were two of the world's
best-looking liners; the Dutch* Nieuw Amsterdam *is
outbound at the right. (Stephen Card Collection).*

Title page: *Marine beauty! The stunningly handsome*
Normandie *is seen in this view at sea by Hayao
Nogami. (Hisashi Noma Collection)*

Front and rear cover images: *(Robert Lloyd)*

## DEDICATION

For Charles Howland –
Dear friend, keen historian and
enthusiast and award-winning
professional.

# CONTENTS

'The first experience can never be repeated,' wrote Robert Louis Stevenson. 'That first love, that first sunrise, that first South Sea island, are memories apart, and touched by a virginity of sense.' And so, in ways, it would be the same for my very first voyage on the largest passenger ship ever created.

Most fortunately, I have sailed aboard over 400 ships and to ports throughout the world. But on January 2011, I had a great treat: to sail aboard the largest ocean liner afloat, the mammoth *Allure of the Seas*. We departed from the world's busiest cruise port, Fort Lauderdale in Florida, for a week in the sun-drenched Caribbean.

Change cruise ships and let's dance! After disembarking from the 92,000-ton, 2,000-bed *Queen Elizabeth* (on a crossing from Southampton to New York and then Florida), we boarded the 225,000-ton, 6,400-passenger *Allure of the Seas*. She's even a tad bigger (just 2 inches actually) than her otherwise twin sister, the *Oasis of the Seas*. So, she makes my record book – she is my very first super mega-liner! The mind boggles, my eyes wide, my imagination deeply tweaked. The 1,187ft-long *Allure* (that's some 50ft longer than the 151,000-ton *Queen Mary 2*), a towering 213ft high, is every inch the 'floating vacation resort'. Yes, a ship that is more – no, much more – than just another 'floating hotel'. Completely, I'm dazzled! But for sure, she could have been named *Colossus of the Seas*.

I'm not alone in being over-impressed. A friend from Florida, who just happens to be aboard, smilingly commented, 'This ship is just magical! It is like another world, a world that is creative and beautiful, but also fantasy-like, even child-like. It is a ship where dreams come true. It is the most remarkable creation ever to sail the seas. And you never, ever feel that there are 6,000 other passengers on board.'

Today, nine liners are 'parked' together in Port Everglades. The 'gang' includes the likes of the *Queen Elizabeth*, *Queen Victoria*, *Celebrity Solstice*, MSC *Poesia* and two Holland America ships among them. It is estimated that well over 20,000 passengers are arriving and, of course, then over 20,000 departing and all before the south Florida sun sets. A new mega-cruise terminal befits the *Allure* and the boarding process takes – with smiles everywhere and quite extraordinarily – just a few minutes. We are whisked through security, checked in at break-neck speed and then cross a glass-tubed gangway and board this behemoth of the seas!

Like some Manhattan skyscraper, we are quickly off to our cabin up on Deck 12 (out of the ship's soaring seventeen decks and said to be equal to a twenty-storey building on shore). Beginning with our Indonesian cabin steward, it is all friendly smiles and chatter and those much needed, helpful directions from step one. Immediately, one senses, the *Allure of the Seas* is not only the biggest liner afloat, but the friendliest! Pure, absolute charm from Royal Caribbean International, the Miami-based owners of the ship and themselves owned by super-rich Norwegian shipowners (the Wilhelmsen Lines) and Chicago-based hoteliers (the Pritzker family and their Hyatt Regency chain)! In total, there's a staggering 2,384 crew on board from no fewer than eighty nations.

ALLURE *of the* SEAS™                    OASIS *of the* SEAS℠

**ALLURE** *of the* **SEAS**
*Inaugural Season*

Our stateroom has a balcony, but one which overlooks the ship's inner core, the vast, open-air courtyard of sorts, that is done decks below as a recreated Central Park. Tree and foliage-lined bliss! Which way to West 72nd Street? After a quick lunch in the massive Windjammer Food Court (with countless serving counters including one just for Thai-Asian) we then stroll along the huge decks (yes, some 'real' exercise, especially in the form of walking, seems to be built in). From the very upper decks, we seem to look down on the 90,000-ton *Queen Victoria*, with her red-orange funnel and aft pool deck, which is docked in the nearest berth.

The public areas on the exceptional *Allure* are meant to be exciting and often very exciting – and they are just that. They are colourfully imaginative feasts to the eye!

◄◄ *The biggest ocean liners of all time, the 225,000-grt sister ships* Allure of the Seas *and* Oasis of the Seas, *seen off Fort Lauderdale in the autumn of 2010, are designed for weekly, seven-day cruises to Caribbean ports. (Royal Caribbean International)*

◄ *The 1,187ft-long* Allure of the Seas *has seventeen decks, twenty-one restaurants, a complete recreation of Central Park as a central open-air well, an ice-skating area, amphitheatre and can accommodate a maximum of 6,400 passengers. (Royal Caribbean International)*

Great applause is due to the designers and interior decorators. It is Disneyland coupled with Disney World coupled with Sea World and all glossed over by the genius of, say, a dozen Las Vegas hotels. One lady from Minnesota said, 'I don't know which way to look next. Everything is so beautiful, so interesting, just so stunning!' A cruise-only travel agent from Florida added, 'I've never seen people more excited about a ship!'

The main ingredients of our evening schedules are prepared, organised and thoughtfully printed out. It becomes our guide. Tonight, it is 'My Time Dining' (with unassigned tables in the huge, three-deck-high main restaurant, but candied by more of that exceptionally friendly Royal Caribbean service) at 5.45p.m.–7.45p.m. and then, walking a 'mile or two or three' to the forward-placed Amber Theatre (yes, more sheer enormity with 2,200 seats) for a ninety-minute production of *Chicago*.

Decorative originality, even splendour! In between, we stroll the Royal Promenade, a long, horizontal promenade area with shops, bars, clubs, yet more eateries and added touches like the gourmet Cupcake Cupboard (yes, there's even cupcake-themed jewellery and handbags) and then to the Boardwalk (pure amusement park with Johnny Rockets, ice cream and hot dog bars, a full merry-go-round and another massive amenity: the 750-seat, open-air Aqua Theatre, located at the very stern of this most unique 'floating resort'). There are jazz and comedy clubs, a huge disco, art gallery, photo studio, make-your-own-stuffed-animal shop, conference room, library, jogging track, internet centre, pizzeria, complete English pub (with dark, rich, wooded interiors), champagne bar, Solera cosmetics emporium, donut and candy shops, Mexican cantina, ice-cream parlour and the very first Starbucks to hit the high seas. You can be certified in scuba, take ice-skating classes, play basketball or miniature golf, join scrapbook-making seminars or enter the Lady Gaga Dress-Up contest.

The ship, which cost $1.5 billion to create, was built in Finland, at the huge STX Europe Shipyard at Turku (which has had to temporarily shut down because of no further orders for new tonnage). The *Allure* is a whopping 208ft wide (almost like one of those monster US Navy aircraft carriers), draws 30ft of water, can speed along at a very respectable 22 knots and has those seventeen passenger decks. Then there are twenty-one restaurants and ten hot tubs, and it takes fifteen to twenty minutes to walk completely around the largest top deck. With great ease and steady comfort, there are twenty-four passenger elevators to cater to a maximum of 6,318 passengers, comfortably housed in no fewer than 2,706 suites and staterooms. The suites include, by the way, duplex lofts, something of a novelty at sea, and sell (at least in a brochure rate) for $14,000 per week for two. However, the average daily, per person rate aboard the *Allure* is a much more affordable $218.

Curtain up! The on-board production of *Chicago* is pure Broadway, with high, high talent and professionalism, and has to be one of the very finest productions I've seen on any ship, anywhere. 'It was magnificent – just perfection,' according to my cabin-mate.

The actors, the dancing, the band and of course that magical score! What a perfect ending to a very exciting first day aboard the *Allure of the Seas*!

The *Allure* is one of the Great Liners. She is in fact the great-great-granddaughter of sorts of the likes of the *Mauretania*, *Imperator*, *Rex*, *Normandie* and the original *Queen Mary*. She is the continuation, the great link, the evolution of passenger ship design as well as ocean travel. In the past century or so, ocean liners have not only continued and grown, but they are more popular than ever. In 2010, more people travelled by ship than at any other time in the history of travel.

Bill Miller
Secaucus, New Jersey
Summer 2011

The story of the Great Liners begins on the Atlantic route between the Old World and the New, between Europe and the United States. It was the most prestigious, most progressive and certainly most competitive ocean liner run of all time. It was on the North Atlantic that the largest, fastest and indeed grandest passenger ships were created. In this book, I am concentrating for the most part on these Atlantic super liners. It has been a race, sometimes fierce, that has continued for well over a century. Smaller passenger ships, even ones of 30,000 and 40,000 tons, are for the most part left to other books.

Our story begins even earlier, in 1889, when Germany's Kaiser Wilhelm II visited his grandmother, Queen Victoria, and attended the British Naval Review at Spithead. The British were more than pleased to show off not only the mightiest naval vessels afloat, but the biggest passenger ships then afloat, namely the 10,000-ton *Teutonic* of the White Star Line. These ships caught the Kaiser's royal eye. His enthusiasm, his determination and, assuredly, his jealousies were aroused. He returned to his homeland determined that Germany should have bigger and better ships. The world must know, he theorised, that Imperial Germany had reached new and higher technological heights. To the Kaiser and other envious Germans, quite simply, the British had had a monopoly on the biggest ships for long enough. British engineers and even shipyard crews were recruited, teaching German shipbuilders the key components of a new generation of larger ships. Shipyards at Bremen, Hamburg and Stettin were soon ready.

It would all take eight years, however, before the first big German liner would be completed. She would be large enough and fast enough to be dubbed the world's first 'super liner'. She would not only be the biggest vessel built in Germany, but the biggest afloat. The nation's most prominent shipowners, the Hamburg America Line and the North German Lloyd, were both deeply interested. It was the Lloyd, however, which rose first to the occasion. Enthusiastically and optimistically, the first ship was the first of a successive quartet. The illustrious Vulkan Shipyard at Stettin was given the prized contract.

Triumph seemed to be in the air! The Kaiser himself went to the launching, on 3 May 1897, of this new Imperial flagship. Designed with four funnels but grouped in pairs, the 655ft-long ship was named *Kaiser Wilhelm der Grosse*, honouring the Emperor's grandfather. With the rattle of chains, the release of the building blocks and then the tumultuous roar as the unfinished hull hit the water, this launching was the beginning of the Atlantic race for supremacy, which would last for some seventy years. Only after the first arrival of the transatlantic jet in October 1958 would the race quieten down. The *Kaiser Wilhelm der Grosse* was the great beginning, the start of a superb fleet of what have been dubbed 'ocean greyhounds' and later aptly called the 'floating palaces'. Worried and cautious, the normally contented British referred to the brand new *Kaiser* as a 'German monster'.

It should be mentioned that back in the 1860s, the large, but very eccentric *Great Eastern* came into service with no fewer

Deutschland
Speisesaal
Hamburg-Amerika Linie

than five funnels. Quite unsuccessful, she is usually not considered to be in the 'Great Liners' category. Her brief commercial career on the Atlantic ended as an 'economic folly' and with her sad demotion as a cable-laying ship.

The *Kaiser Wilhelm der Grosse* was the first liner with four funnels. They towered above the deck, but even more so above the sea. A trend soon started among passengers, especially those souls in lower-deck third class and steerage. The number of funnels, although hardly accurate, was soon equated with a ship's safety, her importance and might. Steamship owners, in Germany and elsewhere, soon noticed that the most popular ships were those with the most 'stacks'. Three-stackers were popular, but four-stackers even more so.

◄ *German décor: The first-class dining room aboard the* Deutschland, *completed in 1900. (Hamburg America Line)*

*Vapore Espresso a doppia elica »Kronprinzessin Cecilie« sulla Piazza S. Pietro a Roma.*
Lunghezza del Vapore 215,34 metri — Larghezza della *Piazza S. Pietro* 198 metri,
Altezza fino ai fumaioli 41 metri — Altezza dell' *Obelisco sulla Piazza* 39 metri.
*Twin-screw Express Mail Steamer "Kronprinzessin Cecilie" on S. Peters Square in Rome.*
Length of Steamer 215,34 meters — Width of *S. Peters Square* 198 meters,
Height of Steamer to the top of funnels 41 meters. — Height of the *Obelisk on the Square* 39 meters.

**Did you know?**
In 1907, 12,000 immigrants were arriving in New York harbour each day and all of them arrived by ship.

◀◀ *Comparative size: the 707ft-long Kronprinzessin Cecilie, one of the world's largest liners when completed in 1906, is compared to St Peter's in Rome. (Author's Collection)*

◀ *Westbound to the New World: 1.5 million immigrants poured into New York during 1907. (Author's Collection)*

18

The *Kaiser Wilhelm der Grosse* was, typically for her time, a three-class ship. There was the marble-clad, gilded, potted palm luxury of upper-deck first class (558 berths in all). Then, slightly less luxurious, was second class (for 338 passengers). But typically, the most profitable was steerage (1,074 berths). Although passengers paid as little as $10 per person for one-way fares from Europe to America, they were 'squeezed' aboard and given the least space, amenity, comfort and food. Ironically, while all the early super liners are well remembered for their luxuries, it was their role as immigrant carriers that earned their greatest profits and most likely paid off their construction costs.

The *Kaiser Wilhelm der Grosse*, which entered service in the autumn of 1897, was praised endlessly. One writer of the day said, 'She is beyond all magnificence. She is all but top heavy with paintings, wood carvings and stained glass. She brought cathedral-like proportions to the traveling public. Alone, she changed the level of luxury on the high seas.' On her maiden crossing, she was also a stunning success for speed, crossing in six days and so snatching the much coveted Blue Riband from Britain's *Lucania*, a Cunarder. It would take the British a full decade to regain the speed honours on the so-called North Atlantic Ferry. It was a nasty blow to Britain, otherwise contented as a great nation, head of a mighty empire and ruler of the seas. It was also Queen Victoria's Jubilee – her sixtieth year as queen-empress. There was only one great blemish for the Germans: the new *Kaiser Wilhelm der Grosse* was soon dubbed 'the Rolling Billy'.

◄ *Once in New York harbour, immigrants were sent to Ellis Island immigration and medical examination. At peak, in 1910, they were arriving at the rate of 12,000 per day. (Ellis Island Museum)*

➤ *Teutonic power and might: the four-funnel, 19,300-grt* Kronprinzessin Cecilie *of 1906 was the largest and fastest ship of any kind. (North German Lloyd)*

Meanwhile, the Hamburg America Line wanted its share and soon commissioned a large, fast liner of its own. She was the *Deutschland*, added in the summer of 1900, weighing in at 16,500 tons and an immediate Blue Riband champion. She held the speed trophy for six years, but at great cost. She proved to be operationally unsound. To maintain her high speed on the Atlantic crossings, she was plagued with vibrations, caused by her high-speed engines, and this was all complicated further by excessive rattling and noise. The peace and tranquillity of her passengers, especially in first class, was greatly disturbed. Passenger numbers fell and she was less than a financial success, in fact the least successful of all Atlantic four-stackers. Hamburg America soon lost interest in high speed and instead

thereafter concentrated on high luxury and on even bigger ships.

North German Lloyd remained interested, however, and produced three more super liners, all of which honoured the German Imperial family. There was the *Kronprinz Wilhelm* in 1901, the *Kaiser Wilhelm II* in 1903 and then the *Kronprinzessin Cecilie* in 1906. Large as well as fast, they were also known for their sumptuous luxuries in first class. There were salons of rich carvings and art treasures, suites and staterooms fitted with marble bathrooms and, aboard the *Kronprinzessin Cecilie*, an 'amazing' four-deck-high light well. These ships were hugely successful, possibly even more so in America, and on her maiden arrival in New York, over 40,000 visitors toured the *Kaiser Wilhelm II*. Fares ranged from $10 in steerage to $2,500 in a lavish suite in first class.

Back across the Channel, the Germans were deeply envied. The White Star Line all but gave up on the subject of speed and instead decided to concentrate on great size. Cunard, however, remained interested in size as well as great speed. They soon prepared a great retaliation to 'those foreigners', the Germans, but planned an experiment first. The British Government promised to assist as well, with generous construction as well as operating subsidies. In 1905, Cunard added two new liners, 20,000-tonners, which were not the largest or grandest, but very important ships just the same. The first of them, the *Carmania*, was fitted with new steam turbines; the second sister, the *Caronia*, had the traditional steam quadruple expansion type. Quickly, the *Carmania* not only proved faster, but more economical to operate. The path was clear – Cunard would build two super liners with steam turbine machinery.

As White Star was now in the hands of American tycoon J.P. Morgan, but while still flying the British flag and thought of as British ships, ministers in London were concerned, even worried, and so supported Cunard through very generous financial support. The two new Cunarders had to be the biggest, fastest, grandest liners on

**Did you know?**

When the *Lusitania* was completed in 1907, she had 175 watertight compartments and was said to be 'as unsinkable as a ship could be'.

**CUNARD LINE**
*Liverpool, New York, Boston* via Queenstown

**Did you know?**

The *Mauretania* of 1907 had a storage capacity for over 6,000 tons of coal. She used 1,000 tons per day for her six-day passages between New York and Liverpool.

◄ *British supremacy: the near-sisters* Lusitania *and* Mauretania *of Cunard were completed in 1907 and became the largest and fastest liners on the Atlantic run between Liverpool and New York. (Cunard Line)*

the Atlantic. They also had to have four funnels just like the Germans. And, with careful planning, they might be useful as giant cruisers or transports in case of war.

Named after Roman provinces in Cunard tradition, the *Lusitania* came first and was named for Roman Portugal; the *Mauretania* followed and drew her name from Roman Morocco. The former was constructed on Scotland's River Clyde, at the John Brown & Co. Shipyard; the second near-sister came

23

CUNARD LINE.

24

from Newcastle, from the yards of Swan, Hunter & Wigham Richardson. Dubbed 'two leviathans of might and speed', they were the very largest ships yet afloat, weighing in at 32,000 tons and some 790ft from stem to stern. They had the likes of ninety-two boilers and 192 furnaces, and consumed 1,000 tons of coal per day. Said to be the most luxuriously appointed liners of their day, their quarters can be seen in the *Mauretania*'s configuration: 560 in first class, 475 in second class and 1,300 in third class-steerage. First class was so lavish that a journalist noted, 'Even the bookcases in the library were copied from originals in the Trianon.' First-class quarters aboard the *Mauretania*, it was said, would 'remind travelers of a stately British country home'.

By the end of 1907, there were seven huge four-stackers on the Atlantic. The Industrial Age, amidst bellowing smoke from factory chimneys and a quest for greater size and increased speed, looked forward. No one, it seemed, was quite satisfied. Cunard, White Star and, of course, the Germans looked to bigger and bigger ships. Cunard planned one while White Star and Hamburg America were even more ambitious with sets of three liners each. While first-class travellers loved the grandeur and elegance of the biggest liners, those down in lower-deck third class preferred them for their expected smoothness at sea, fast passages and, most of all, safe passage across the otherwise 'treacherous North Atlantic'. Cunard's *Lusitania* and *Mauretania* firmly established the era of the turbine-driven super liner and also created the generation of the 'floating palace'.

◄ *Sea-going splendour: the first-class main lounge aboard the 2,165-passenger* Lusitania. *(Cunard Line)*

**Did you know?**
The lavish quarters on the *Lusitania* and *Mauretania* prompted the term 'floating palaces'.

White Star Line was next in the queue, it seems, with designs for three giant ships: the projected *Olympic* and *Titanic* as sisters and then, even slightly larger, the *Gigantic* as a one-off. Each was designed to be the biggest as well as the most splendid liner on the Atlantic, but not the fastest. Constructed at the Harland & Wolff shipyard at Belfast, the public was fascinated by the first of these behemoths, the 45,000-ton *Olympic*, when she was launched in October 1910. She would be, it was reported, the most luxurious liner of all time with her Louis Seize dining room 114ft long and seating 532 persons at one time and the first 'plunge bath' (swimming pool) ever to go to sea. Then there was later mention of her 'exotic Turkish bath with cooling rooms in the style of seventeenth-century Arabia and hinting

*▶ Bigger and bigger: in 1911, the White Star Line, arch rival to Cunard, began a series of three larger liners: the* Olympic, Titanic *and* Britannic. *(Author's Collection)*

WHITE STAR    LMS
*The Big Ship Route*    *The Best Way*
★ BY SEA ★    BY LAND

of the grandeurs of the mysterious East'. Some writers began to suggest that these extremely comfortable, amenity-filled ships were in fact destinations in themselves.

White Star was very keen on publicity and so, on 31 May 1911, cleverly had the second ship, the *Titanic*, launched at noon and as guests then boarded the brand new *Olympic* that afternoon for her overnight delivery cruise from Belfast to Southampton. Two four-stackers and the world's largest liners in one day – what could be more impressive!

While the *Olympic* settled down to a long, productive career, the *Titanic* would become the most famous ship of all time. No ship has ever had such widespread celebrity – the subject of hundreds of books, thousands of articles, countless film and television documentaries, some 100 songs and hundreds of poems, a Broadway musical and Hollywood's first billion-dollar blockbuster movie (called *Titanic* and premiered in 1997).

White Star, worried that she would not get adequate publicity or attention, took Harland & Wolff's notation of added steel reinforcement and compartmentalisation, and soon proclaimed the liner as the 'world's very first unsinkable ship'. Consequently, she was completed with too few lifeboats

**Did you know?**
The *Olympic* of 1911 had the first indoor pool to go to sea.

**Did you know?**
The final funnels, either the third or fourth, on many liners were actually 'dummy stacks' and were used by immigrant passengers as an indication of size, might and therefore safety.

*Disaster: unfortunately, the brand new, 'unsinkable' Titanic actually sank and on her maiden voyage no less, in April 1912. Over 1,500 perished. (James Sesta Collection)*

and even life-saving equipment for her full complement of 2,600 passengers and 900 staff and crew.

The maiden westbound crossing from Southampton to New York of the *Titanic* has been well documented. Suffice to say that while en route, just before midnight on 14 April 1912, she sideswiped an iceberg that ripped a 300ft-long gash in her starboard side. The cut was fatal and the ship doomed. Two and a half hours later, the liner sank in a position 380 miles east of Newfoundland in 12,000ft of cold North Atlantic water. An estimated 1,522 passengers and crew were lost. Just after 4a.m., the first rescue ship (Cunard's *Carpathia*) arrived and began receiving the 705 survivors or approximately 32 per cent of all those who had been aboard the tragic *Titanic*. It was the worst sea disaster up to that date. White Star itself never fully recovered and, to some, it was seen as the beginning of the end of the Britain's vast empire and its contented supremacy.

The *Gigantic* was larger than both the *Olympic* and *Titanic*, but a most unfortunate ship in her own right. She was to complete the three-liner express service between Southampton and New York for White Star. In the wake of the *Titanic* tragedy, she was renamed, less pretentiously, as *Britannic* and was due in service in 1915. The First World War had started the year before, in August 1914, and instead the 903ft-long liner was completed directly as a wartime hospital ship. Sadly, she lasted but a year, sinking in the Aegean on 21 November 1916. In a short time, White Star had lost two of its three new super liners.

**Did you know?**
The *Titanic* was
promoted as
the 'world's first
unsinkable ship'. She is
also the most famous
liner of all time.

The enthusiastic fever for creating bigger and grander liners spread to the French in the wake of big Cunard and White Star tonnage. In 1909, they ordered their first (and only) four-stacker, to be called *La Picardie*, but then renamed *France*. Topped by her quartet of red and black funnels, she set off for New York for the first time in May 1912, just weeks after the *Titanic* went to the bottom. She wasn't the biggest or fastest, but one of the best decorated and certainly one of the best fed (eighteen barrels of paté de foie gras were trundled aboard, for example). The four-class *France* was said to embody the finest styles of French décor and was soon dubbed 'the Chateau of the Atlantic'. Her public rooms were grand, her dining room fitted with a sweeping stairwell as an entrance and, in the evenings at sea, passengers could pass the time in the Moorish salon which included a fountain under an Algerian fresco and attended by exotic North African stewards. The *France* was so successful that it prompted the French Line (the Compagnie Generale Transatlantique), her owners, to build a successively larger, more luxurious liner every four years.

➤ *French style: the four-funnel* France *of 1912 was the first of the French Line's great liners. (Author's Collection)*

**Did you know?**

The *Ile de France* of 1927 was said to have 'the longest bar afloat' and the best ambience of any Atlantic liner. She was also said to be the best fed, with 275 items on her first-class dinner menus.

*French line*

By 1910, the Germans, namely the Hamburg America Line, were more than anxious to surpass the new generation of British super liners. In high enthusiasm, they would produce the biggest, most extravagant Atlantic liners yet. The initial keel plates for the first of these ships, already dubbed 'the colossus of the Atlantic,' were laid in June 1910. Excitement prevailed at her birthplace in a Hamburg shipyard while workers over in Belfast had started on the first of White Star's projected trio, the *Olympic*. The ocean liner world was preparing for the greatest and grandest ships yet built. While the *Olympic* would be 45,000 tons and the projected *Aquitania* of Cunard (due in 1914) placed at 46,000 tons , the first of the Germans, thought to be named *Europa*, would be 'at least' 52,000 tons. Launched by the Kaiser in

May 1912, just five weeks after the *Titanic* sank, this mammoth, 919ft-long ship was actually named *Imperator*. She would be capped by three funnels, the tallest yet fitted to a liner and rising 69ft above the upper deck. There were accommodations for 4,594 passengers, no fewer than eighty-three lifeboats and two motor launches, and bunkers for 8,500 tons of coal. She was completed in the spring of 1913 and soon sent off to New York. Immediately, she was the great symbol of Germany's technological as well as maritime might. The Kaiser himself was thrilled and delighted.

There was one noted blemish for the new flagship, however. She was top heavy, listed even in port and sometimes rolled so deeply at sea that she not only terrified passengers but the crew as well. Drastic changes were soon made. The height of her

33

▶ *Stars and Stripes!*
*The mighty, 950ft-long*
Leviathan *was America's*
*only super liner in the*
*1920s and '30s. (United*
*States Lines)*

funnels were soon shortened, ponderous ornamental furnishings were removed and even the marble bathtubs in first class reduced. But further steps were needed – such as putting 2,000 tons of concrete in her bottom. In the end, she remained a 'slightly clumsy and very fragile ship'.

The German plan was to build successively larger liners and so the second of the class, also to have been named *Europa*, but finally christened *Vaterland* (at her launch in April 1913), exceeded 54,000 tons and was more than 30ft longer than the first ship. In fact, the 950ft-long *Vaterland* had to be immediately stopped once launched at Hamburg for fear of otherwise ramming the opposite side of the River Elbe. Everything, or so it seemed, was bigger and greater on these German titans. The crew on the similar-sized *Aquitania* was fixed at

970, for example, but on the *Vaterland* it was set at 1,234. She also had sixty chefs working in her eight kitchens and the largest 'black gang', the coal stokers, over 400 in all, at sea. Everything about seemed beyond imagination: 14,000 napkins used on a week-long crossing, 45,000lb of meat, 100,000lb of potatoes and 28,000 litres of German beer. Of course, she had every amenity: a winter garden, grill room, entire row of shops, a bank, a travel bureau and a lower deck 'complex' of swimming pool and gymnasium. Her first-class quarters were headed by a pair of luxurious imperial suites. Her safety components were then the finest at sea: a twenty-four-hour wireless telegraph system, strengthened hull plating, a huge searchlight on the foredeck and the finest fire prevention system then afloat. Sadly, the new *Vaterland* saw very little service. Commissioned in May 1914, she was laid-up, at Hoboken, within the confines of New York harbour, when war in Europe began that August. She would never again sail for the Germans.

The third big German, the *Bismarck*, never even entered Hamburg-America Line service. Launched in June 1914, war started just six weeks later. The largest of all, at 56,500 tons, she sat idle and incomplete through the conflict and then was ceded to the British as reparations.

**Did you know?**
When completed in 1913, the *Imperator* could carry more passengers than any other big liner on the Atlantic.

➤ *Maritime perfection: The 45,600-grt, 3,230-passenger* Aquitania, *completed in 1914, was ocean liner ideal on the inside as well as the out. She was dubbed 'the Ship Beautiful'. (Cunard Line)*

Three big, fast, luxurious liners were needed by Atlantic shipping companies to maintain a weekly 'express service'. It took seven years for Cunard to add a proper running-mate to the team of *Lusitania* and *Mauretania*. This third ship, named *Aquitania* (for Roman France) was larger and of elaborate design. Commissioned in the spring of 1914, again all but on the eve of the First World War, the handsome lines of her exterior were matched with the high beauty of her interiors. She was soon dubbed 'the Ship Beautiful'. To many, she had some of the finest public rooms on all the seas: the Carolean smoking room, Palladian lounge, Louis XVI restaurant and Jacobean grill room. Her indoor pool was decorated with replicas of ancient Egyptian ornaments.

The First World War threw the great liners into disarray, even havoc. Those

◄ *The wonderful Georgian lounge aboard the* Aquitania *in a special auto chrome view by Joseph B. Rayder and Eric K. Longo. (Eric Longo Collection)*

▲ *Country house on the high seas: the Carolean smoke room, aboard the grand* Aquitania. *(Eric Longo Collection)*

**Did you know?**

Many thought that Cunard's *Aquitania* was the best-decorated liner of her time.

▲ *The exquisite Louis XVI Restaurant, the first-class dining room, also aboard the 24-knot* Aquitania. *(Eric Longo Collection)*

SOUTHAMPTON

GREAT BRITAIN'S PREMIER DOCKS
owned and managed by the
SOUTHERN RAILWAY OF ENGLAND
For all information, write Docks Manager, Southampton, England.

◄ *Spectacle! Liners in a floating dry dock, such as the 56,500-grt Majestic, created indelible impressions to the public. They seemed bigger and taller and longer than expected! (Author's Collection)*

initial Germans had varied fates: the *Kaiser Wilhelm der Grosse* was sunk early in the war, in 1914, while the other three, the *Kronprinz Wilhelm*, *Kaiser Wilhelm II* and *Kronprinzessin Cecilie* fell into American hands. The troublesome former *Deutschland* was left with the Germans, however, but was only restored as a much-demoted immigrant ship, the *Hansa*, in 1920. The *Mauretania* would sail on, as beloved and as popular as ever, until given over to scrappers in Scotland in 1935. The *Olympic* finished her days at the breakers as well, but in 1936. The *France* also had a long life, ending up at the scrappers in 1935. The three giant Germans became reparations of war with the *Imperator* becoming the *Berengaria* for Cunard, the *Vaterland* changing to *Leviathan* for the United States Lines and finally the incomplete *Bismarck* was handed over to White Star, who renamed her *Majestic*. Finally, the *Aquitania* had the longest career of all – she sailed for thirty-five years until retired and broken up in 1950.

**Did you know?**
When she was retired in 1949, the *Aquitania*
was the very last four-funnel liner.

Following the First World War and well into the first half of the 1920s, creating super liners was put on hold, it seemed. More moderate-sized tonnage was the order of the day. One of the first new, large liners was the 43,100-ton *Ile de France*, completed in 1927. She was a follow-up to the earlier *France*, but with a significant change: her décor was new and different, modernist and based on the 1925 Exposition of Art and Decoration in Paris. It was, in fact, the beginning of Art Deco on the high seas, 'ocean liner style' as it was also dubbed. It ignored the dark woods and heavy gilding of the past, but used lighter woods and colours, sleek and angular designs, and added touches such as tubular chairs and soft, indirect lighting. Other liners quickly

◄ *French style! The lighted* Paris, *romantic and alluring, ploughs through North Atlantic seas in this poster from the 1920s. Liners were the ultimate symbols of great speed. (French Line)*

*◄◄ Sea-going style! By the 1920s, the great comforts and luxuries of life aboard the great ocean liners were alluring to the public. (French Line)*

*◄ New look! After the Second World War, the celebrated* Ile de France *returned to service (in 1949), but modernised, improved and – like in Parisian fashion – with a new look: two instead of three funnels. She is seen here, departing from New York, viewed from the stern of the* Queen Elizabeth. *(Frank Andrews Collection)*

followed the immensely popular *Ile de France*, and later so did hotels, department stores, skyscrapers, railway terminals and Hollywood set designers. It was later called 'floating Ginger Rogers'.

The *Ile* had it all, so it seemed – the longest bar then afloat, a Parisian pavement café and even a real carousel (with painted ponies) in the children's playroom. Each of her 439 first-class staterooms was fitted out in a different décor and, carrying more first-class passengers than any other Atlantic liner by the early '30s, the French Line noted there were also 'four apartments of great luxury and ten of luxury'. The first-class dining room, three decks in height, was one of 'massive simplicity' and likened to being like a 'modern Greek temple'. The cuisine was, of course, exceptional and unsurpassable. It was quite true: 'More sea gulls followed the French liners than any other ships!'

**Did you know?**

When she was retired in 1959, the *Ile de France* spent her final weeks as a floating prop in the Hollywood film *The Last Voyage*.

After the defeat and losses during the First World War, the Germans gradually returned and revived their liner fleet. The first new, large liner, completed in 1924, was the 32,500-ton *Columbus*. Her North German Lloyd owners also planned two near-sisters, but then expanded ideas to a pair of very fast, more luxurious, 50,000-tonners instead. They would, it was estimated, take the Blue Riband from

**Did you know?**

The German *Bremen* introduced the bulbous bow in 1929, a rounded underwater stem that greatly reduced drag at sea.

◀ *The Deco Age! By the late 1920s, the great age of Art Deco dawned over the world of ocean liners. North German Lloyd began to promote their brand new super liners* Bremen *and* Europa *with imaginative, highly stylised art. (North German Lloyd)*

◀◀ *German might! The* Bremen *encounters fierce Atlantic weather, but continues onward and on schedule in this superb painting by Japanese artist Hayao Nogami. (Hisashi Noma Collection)*

◀ *Well stacked! Soon after their completion, the funnels aboard the* Bremen *and* Europa *were heightened for improved smoke emission. Stacks aboard ships were equated with size, speed and safety. (North German Lloyd)*

*➤ Art form! In this splendid poster, North German Lloyd's three-ship express service – with the* Bremen, Europa *and* Columbus *– is promoted to the Czech market. (Richard Faber Collection)*

*➤➤ Bon voyage! Advertising art was used to 'transport' prospective passengers to the glories and excitements of ocean liner travel. Few aspects were more exciting and appealing than a ship's departure, that romantic and poetic sense of bon voyage. (Norman Knebel Collection)*

**Did you know?**

The German flagship *Bremen* hoisted the Soviet colours for a short time in late 1939 to avoid attack and capture by the British.

Cunard's enduring *Mauretania*. Named *Bremen* and *Europa*, the ships were launched a day apart, in August 1928, and were rumoured to have simultaneous maiden crossings to New York. In high enthusiasm, they were to capture the Blue Riband together! But plans went astray when the nearly complete *Europa* caught fire at a Hamburg shipyard in March 1929 and was very nearly destroyed. The *Bremen* entered service on schedule, that July, but the *Europa* needed extensive repairs and was delayed by a year. Both ships captured the Blue Riband and made Germany very proud. Alone, the *Bremen's* record stood at four days, seventeen hours.

While their original squat funnels had to be doubled in height because of soot

49

problems on the upper passenger decks, they introduced the bulbous bow, a knife-like stem that substantially reduced drag. They also carried a Lufthansa seaplane resting in a revolving catapult on the very upper deck. Some thirty-six hours before reaching either side of the Atlantic, priority bags of mail were sent ahead by air and thereby well in advance of the ship itself. A noteworthy, publicity-making scheme, it did prove costly and awkward, and so was discontinued by 1935.

➤ *The 42,500-grt Empress of Britain was the largest liner ever created for transatlantic service to Canada. (Canadian Pacific Steamships)*

The North Atlantic run to Eastern Canada instead of New York warranted many smaller and medium-sized passenger ships, but only one super liner: the *Empress of Britain* of Canadian Pacific Steamships, a ship commissioned in 1931. Capped by three oversized funnels and having an all-white hull, she was the grandest, largest and fastest liner ever to sail between Southampton and Quebec City. In winter, she had an alternate purpose: four-month-

**Did you know?**

The outer propellers on the *Empress of Britain* of 1931 would be removed each winter in preparation for the ship's more leisurely world cruise.

EMPRESS OF BRITAIN
42,350 TONS · FIVE DAY CROSSING

*Canadian Pacific*
WORLD'S GREATEST TRAVEL SYSTEM

long, luxury cruises around the world. She had superb accommodations, of course: columned lounges, a main lounge done in Greek styling, luxurious suites and staterooms, and the very first large tennis court afloat on her top decks.

**Did you know?**
Personal servants could accompany passengers for $1,200 on the *Empress of Britain*'s 125-day around-the-world cruises in the 1930s.

◄ *Dominated by three very large 'gas tank' funnels, the 748ft-long* Empress of Britain *was one of the great examples of a great ocean liner. She is seen here, well underway, in a splendid painting by Japan's Hayao Nogami. (Hisashi Noma Collection)*

**Did you know?**

The *Rex*, the 1932-built flagship of Italy, was to have been named *Guglielmo Marconi*.

Mussolini and his Fascist ministers wanted their share of the ocean liner business and so created two super liners, the *Rex* and *Conte di Savoia*, in 1932. They would offer the first 'big ship' service on the mid-Atlantic, to and from Mediterranean ports. Their expected festive maiden crossings to America were embarrassing

➤ *Italian record-breaker! Hayao Nogami also painted the largest and fastest of Italy's Atlantic liners, the* Rex *of 1932. (Hisashi Noma Collection)*

54

SERVIZI PER LE AMERICHE

failures, however. While westbound to New York on her inaugural crossing, the *Rex* broke down with mechanical problems at Gibraltar. Delayed and with fewer passengers, she limped to her Manhattan destination, but then needed power from a floating tender. Two months later, in November, on her maiden crossing, an outlet valve below the waterline jammed aboard the *Conte di Savoia*. A sizeable hole erupted in the hull of the 48,500-ton ship, there was subsequent flooding and, it

was estimated, she might sink in five hours. Fortunately, due to the near superhuman efforts of her crew, temporary repairs were made by plugging the hole with cement and then the 818ft-long *Conte di Savoia* was able to continue to New York.

Both the *Rex* and *Conte di Savoia* had lavish lounges, superb dining and the first outdoor pools aboard super liners. With striped umbrellas and even using sand on the decks, the Italians cleverly borrowed a name from Venice and called this outdoor pool area the Lido Deck. It was also described as being 'the Riviera Afloat'.

◄ *The second of Italy's large 1930s super liners, the 48,500-grt* Conte di Savoia, *is seen here in a painting by Bermuda-based artist Stephen Card. (Stephen Card Collection)*

**Did you know?**
The *Conte di Savoia* of 1932 was dubbed 'the roll-less ship' because of the very first use on a big liner of a new gyro-stabiliser system.

Without question, France's *Normandie* was the most glamorous and superbly decorated Atlantic super liner. Her exceptional $60 million cost ($900 million in 2011 dollars), heavily underwritten by the French Government, also made her the most costly liner of her time. She was planned as the largest, fastest and grandest

▶ *French sensation! Departing from her home port of Le Havre, the exquisite 1935-built* Normandie *is seen here in Albert Brenet's brilliant painting. (French Line)*

▶▶ *Maiden arrival! Albert Brenet also painted the* Normandie's *maiden arrival in New York harbour in 1935. (French Line)*

*Romantic nights! The lighted* Normandie *was perhaps even more alluring in a night view than in daylight. (French Line)*

**Did you know?**

The main dining room on the *Normandie* rose three decks in height, sat 1,000 guests and was longer than the Hall of Mirrors at Versailles.

ship, but also as a showcase for 'the genius of France'. She was floating ambassador, grand flag-waver, but also floating hotel and even floating museum. The very finest designers and decorators in all France would contribute to this maritime tour de force. However, Vladimir Yourkevitch, a former designer of Russian Imperial battleships, was placed in charge of the project, creating her advanced overall design and exterior. She was exceptional in every way: the first liner to exceed 75,000 tons and the first to surpass 1,000ft in length. Names such as Neptune, General Pershing, La Belle France, Napoleon, Jeanne d'Arc and even Maurice Chevalier were suggested before *Normandie* was finally selected. Launched at Chantiers de l'Atlantique at St-Nazaire in western France in October 1932, the ship already had a sense of the dramatic: 100 workmen were swept into the Loire at launching. With her final construction halted for a time due to the Depression, she was finally completed and entered service between Le Havre, Southampton and New York in May 1935. The maiden voyage broke all records: 32 knots at full speed and with a passage of four days and three hours.

On board, she was beyond impressive and certainly wondrous. Her main restaurant, done in bronze, hammered glass and Lalique, was longer than the Hall of Mirrors at Versailles and offered some 300 items as a dinner menu. The bronze doors outside led to a vestibule lined with Algerian onyx. There was an indoor pool of 100ft of tiered, lighted levels and a winter garden complete with fresh greenery and live birds. There was a chapel, the first cinema to go to sea, an extensive library, a grill room, various salons and the very finest suites and penthouses on the Atlantic. The top penthouses even had their own music rooms and private dining salons. Otherwise, in first class, no two cabins were alike – including one creation in Louis XIV and another in red lacquer. Even the dog kennel had its own sun deck. There was a flower shop, chocolate shop and an on-board tailor that could prepare a man's suit within the usual five-day crossings.

**Did you know?**
All of the first-class cabins on the *Normandie*, 400 in all, were fitted out in a different décor.

**Did you know?**
The most lavish apartments on board the *Normandie* included a private terrace, four bedrooms, a living room with piano, private dining room and up to five bathrooms.

◄ *Eight courses! The main dining room aboard the* Normandie *was longer than Hall of Mirrors at Versailles. (Richard Faber Collection)*

◄ *Refuge! The Winter Garden aboard the* Normandie, *with live birds and fresh greenery, was a refuge and retreat on grey, even stormy Atlantic passages. (Richard Faber Collection)*

▶ Quiet and empty! The grand Normandie was laid up at New York in the late summer of 1939, just as war clouds were mounting in Europe. (French Line)

▶▶ Manhattan limbo! In the autumn and winter of 1939–40, several of the great liners waited at New York for a call to war duties. Here, in a view from September 1939, we see (from left to right) the Aquitania, Queen Mary, Normandie and Ile de France. (Author's Collection)

There were plans, in 1938, of building a 'super Normandie', another advanced design but of some 90,000 tons and named Bretagne, but plans were scrapped, partly because of cost, but mostly the approaching war in Europe. The Normandie herself was a great success for the image of France, but was not an economic winner. Because of her exceptional luxuries and image, she inhibited many 'ordinary passengers' and so sailed only at 59 per cent of capacity in her four years of service, until August 1939. With the exception of the Queen Mary, all of the big, new super liners of the 1930s were less than economically successful. The Bremen and Europa carried fewer passengers because of lingering anti-German feelings left over from the First World War and then, by the mid-1930s, increasing anti-Nazi sentiments. The Empress of Britain was

◄◄ *Fierce flames! The beautiful but tragic* Normandie *burns to death at Pier 88 in New York on 9 February 1942. (Author's Collection)*

◄ *Salvage! Cut-down and slowly being righted, the remains of the 1,028ft-long* Normandie *are seen in this view from the summer of 1943. (Author's Collection)*

➤ *Bound for the breakers! The powerless hull of the great* Normandie *is towed to the scrappers' yard at Port Newark in New Jersey in this view from November 1946. (Author's Collection)*

**Did you know?**

When the $60 million *Normandie* was sold for scrap in 1946, the burnt-out, cut-down liner fetched only $161,000.

simply too big for the Canadian run and the mid-Atlantic service to the Mediterranean for the *Rex* and *Conte di Savoia* had yet to fully catch on.

The exquisite *Normandie* was laid up in August 1939 at New York, owing to the uncertainty of the political situation in Europe, never to sail again.

In the late 1920s, to reinforce Britain's position amidst the 'super-liner sweep-stakes', Cunard ordered an 80,000-ton liner from John Brown on the Clyde while White Star planned for a 60,000-tonner from Harland & Wolff at Belfast. To be named *Victoria* and *Oceanic*, they were to be operated as a two-ship team on the premier service between Southampton and New York. But the sinister Depression wreaked havoc – both companies lost millions in the early 1930s, as the Atlantic liner trade slumped from 1 million passengers a year in 1930 to 500,000 by 1935. The White Star project was abandoned and the new Cunarder delayed, sitting idle for 2½ years at Clydebank. When construction did resume in April 1934, supported by huge loans and operating subsidies from the British Government, the naming created

a curious story. In a meeting with King George V and the Cunard chairman, the

◀ *Great, inspiring and often exotic advertising art flourished in the 1930s and this was due in large part to the age of the great liners. (Author's Collection)*

**Did you know?**

There were no fewer than fifty-six kinds of wood used in the decoration of the *Queen Mary*.

70

King was said to have misunderstood about using his grandmother's name, but instead responded with 'my wife will be delighted and I'll tell her tonight'. His wife was *Queen Mary* and so the naming held. Their Majesties travelled to the John Brown yard for the naming and launch in September 1934.

◄◄ *The design and décor of the great 1930s skyscrapers was greatly influenced by the great ocean liners. The 1929-built Chrysler Building dominates this night-time view of Midtown Manhattan. (Author's Colldection)*

◄ *Canine luxury! Even dogs lived the grand life aboard the great liners – there were recreations of New York City fire hydrants and even tasseled pet menus on some of the biggest ships. Here we see an afternoon stroll aboard the* Queen Mary. *(Cunard Line)*

**Did you know?**

During the Second World War, the *Queen Mary* left New York in July 1943 with 16,683 soldier-passengers and crew on board. This is the greatest record ever for any ship.

# R.M.S. QUEEN MARY

## SOUTHAMPTON - NEW YORK

The 81,000-ton *Queen Mary* came into service in the spring of 1936 and immediately was the greatest rival to France's *Normandie*. While the French flagship was more innovative and certainly more lavish, the *Queen Mary* was a great success, sailing in her first years at 98 per cent of capacity. There were rivalries between the two in speed, contests for the prized Blue Riband, but the Cunarder finally won out and firmly took the record with a crossing of 31.6 knots – three days and twenty-one hours. In another contest, the *Queen Mary* was larger, which so displeased the French that the *Normandie* was rushed into dry dock during her first winter and given an otherwise useless deckhouse, which raised her tonnage to 82,800, or 1,400 tons greater than the Cunard flagship.

Cunard's second super liner, biggest of all at 83,600 tons and named *Queen Elizabeth*, was due in the much-anticipated, twin-liner New York–Southampton express service in April 1940. Named by HM Queen Elizabeth (later the Queen Mother) at her launching in September 1938, the outbreak of war in Europe in September 1939 changed everything. A gala maiden crossing for the 1,031ft-long *Elizabeth*, the world's largest as well as longest liner, was cancelled and instead the ship crossed to America in grey war-paint and was soon conscripted for trooping duties.

The *Queen Mary* and *Queen Elizabeth* were the most heroic troopships of all time, together ferrying 2 million soldiers across the Atlantic between 1942 and 1945. They were refitted to carry some 15,000 soldier-passengers per crossing. In fact, the *Queen Mary*, built to carry some 2,000 in comfortable peacetime accommodations, established the greatest record for any passenger ship when she departed New York in July 1943 with 16,683 on board. While hundreds of other passenger ships

**Did you know?**
When the *Queen Mary* was retired from active service in 1967, she had made over 1,000 crossings on the Atlantic and ranked as the last three-funnel liner.

participated in wartime service and duty, Winston Churchill said that the efforts of the two Queens alone helped to shorten the war in Europe by at least a year.

By the war's end in the summer of 1945, many of the great super liners were gone. The otherwise hard-pressed years of the 1930s Depression were especially tough on the older super liners, those 'floating palaces' from before the First World War. Aged and so less profitable, the *Mauretania*, *Olympic*, *France*, *Berengaria* (ex-*Imperator*), *Leviathan* (ex-*Vaterland*) and *Majestic* (ex-*Bismarck*) all found their way to the breakers. Some ships left service prematurely. The *Majestic*, the largest liner afloat prior to the *Normandie*, had in fact only sailed fourteen years in all. Later, and while the Cunard Queens were valiant, heroic, highly successful troopships during the Second

'QUEEN ELIZABETH'

THE WORLD'S LARGEST LINER

CUNARD    WHITE    STAR

World War and then later revived, the other great liners suffered destructive fates. The *Empress of Britain*, *Bremen*, *Normandie*, *Rex* and *Conte di Savoia* were all casualties; the *Ile de France* survived while the German *Europa* was eventually ceded to the French as reparations and sailed as their *Liberté* until scrapped in 1962.

The Queens were the most popular pair of liners on the Atlantic run following the Second World War. They were usually booked to capacity and earned millions. Typical of a five-night crossing for these giant Cunarders was the likes of $75,000 worth of express, high-quality cargo in the holds, 650 bags of mail, three dozen diplomatic pouches, 1,500 bon voyage parcels, 1,700 pieces of heavy baggage, 9,000 pieces of stateroom baggage, two dozen cars, over 100 containers of cinema

**Did you know?**
The *Queen Elizabeth* had to make a secret, fast dash to the safety of America in March 1940. Her actual commercial maiden crossing had to wait for over six years, until October 1946.

➤ *It was $120 for first class in high summer in the late 1930s to make a five-night crossing on the brand new* Queen Mary. *(Cunard Line)*

➤➤ *Dining in splendour! The first-class dining room aboard the* Queen Mary *was three decks high. (Author's Collection)*

film, nearly 500 bars of gold bullion and two dozen dogs. Divided into three classes, there were fares in the 1950s from $400 for the five-day crossing in first class, $250 in cabin class and from $175 in tourist class. Top-deck suites were priced from $1,200 and dogs crossed in the ship's kennels for $25. Reserving a deck chair was put at $1.75

while dining in the exclusive Verandah Grill in first class had an added charge of $12.

There were the occasional mishaps, those disruptions to otherwise well-planned schedules, of course. In April 1947, the *Queen Elizabeth* ran aground in the Solent as she approached Southampton. Numerous tugs were called out to assist in refloating the largest liner in the world. The *Queen Mary* was tossed about in one of the worst storms ever recorded in March 1956. Some forty passengers and fifty crew members were injured. Three years later, in August 1959, in a thick summer haze, the *Queen Elizabeth* collided with a freighter in the outer reaches of New York harbour. The smaller ship was said to have 'bounced off' the giant Cunarder.

Liner service between Europe and America reached its peak by the mid-1950s. New liners, even from the likes of Greece, Portugal, Spain and Israel, came into regular service. But commercial jets were a new, devastating competitor after the inaugural flights in the autumn of 1958. Increasingly, the liners lost passengers and consequently fell on hard economic times. On one voyage in the early 1960s, the mighty *Queen Elizabeth* arrived in New York with 175 passengers and all being looked after by 1,200 crew. It had all become a huge money-losing operation. One by one, the liners sailed off into either attempted revivals as tropical cruise ships, but mostly to scrap yards. The *Queen Mary* was retired, after thirty-one years of service and 1,000 crossings, in September 1967, but found further life as a moored hotel and museum ship at Long Beach, California. The *Queen Elizabeth* was not

**Did you know?**
Winston Churchill said that as giant troopships, the efforts of the *Queen Mary* and *Queen Elizabeth* helped to bring forward the end of the war in Europe by at least a year.

► *The Queen Mary was decorated with fifty-six kinds of genuine woods, all of them from parts of the then-vast British Empire. (Cunard Line)*

►► *Valiant service! During the Second World War, both Queens were heroic, highly useful troopships. They often carried over 15,000 soldier-passengers per crossing between 1942 and 1945. (Author's Collection)*

➤ *During the Second World War, there were eight sessions of breakfast, twenty minutes each, aboard the grey-painted* Queen Elizabeth *(seen here) and* Queen Mary. *(Cunard Line)*

➤➤ *In July 1943, the* Queen Mary *established the all-time record of any ship when she departed from New York with 16,683 on board. (Cunard Line)*

as fortunate. After a misplaced attempt to use her as a hotel-museum as well, but at Fort Lauderdale, Florida, she was auctioned off to a Chinese shipping tycoon, renamed *Seawise University* and was to be used in educational-style cruising. Most unfortunately, she caught fire in Hong Kong harbour, in January 1972, on the eve of her first voyage. She was ruined, capsized and then had to be cut up for scrap. By 1975, all of the Atlantic super liners had left service with the exception of the *Queen Elizabeth 2*.

### Did you know?
The *Queen Elizabeth* was the largest liner ever built, a record held until as recently as 1996.

When the Second World War ended, Atlantic liner travel resumed. The Cold War set in, however, and America was worried about the possibility of a Third World War. Therefore, Washington generously contributed and the Pentagon virtually controlled the design and construction of a giant troopship that was disguised as a big

➤ *Yankee might! Planned in the late 1940s, the brilliant* United States *was intended to be the most powerful ocean liner ever created. (United States Lines)*

liner. She was, in fact, the most advanced ship of her time. Built under strict secrecy and named *United States*, she was floated out (rather than launched) in June 1951 and then ready for service twelve months later. It was later revealed that during her sea trials, in the spring of 1952, that the 53,000-tonner managed 43 knots for a time and also did a full 20 knots in reverse. On her maiden crossing to England, she swept the Atlantic forever with speeds of 39 knots. Built to the specifications of a warship, she was said to be so fireproof that the only wood aboard was in the butcher's block in the kitchen and in the Steinway piano in the lounge. It was said that she could be converted with days from a 2,000-capacity liner to a 15,000-plus capacity troop transport. She had an abnormally large fuel capacity, subdivisions of watertight compartments

◀ *The 990ft-long ship was officially named in ceremonies at Newport News, Virginia, in June 1951. (United States Lines)*

**Did you know?**
During her sea trials in 1952, the *United States* reached a top speed of 43 knots as well as 20 knots in reverse.

and a distribution of machinery that would allow for the operation of the 990ft-long ship even if part of the ship was under attack. More aluminium was built in her than any other structure on land or sea. An enormous success, she sailed at over 95 per cent of capacity in her first decade of service.

➤ Swift crossings! *The* United States *was only late four times in seventeen years due to her extraordinary speed capacity and consequent ability to make-up time if delayed by bad weather or thick fog. (United States Lines)*

➤➤ *European popularity! The* United States *was especially popular with North European passengers who, it was said, wanted to experience 'something of the American way of life'. (Author's Collection)*

Southampton Docks OCEAN TERMINAL opened in 1950, replaced the sheds originally built in

◄ *In port! The* United States *made regular five-day crossings between New York, Le Havre and Southampton (where the 990ft-long liner is seen in this advertising poster). On some voyages, in six days, she continued to Bremerhaven in Germany. (Port of Southampton Authority)*

**Did you know?**

The *United States* sailed for seventeen years, but has been idle for forty-two years.

The *United States* had seventeen years of service before, in November 1969, the US Government revoked her much-needed operating subsidy. She has been laid-up ever since, for forty-two years (by 2011), which have encompassed schemes to remake her as a hotel, motel, trade ship, hospital ship and of course a revived liner, especially for current day cruising. Faded, rusting and all but completely gutted on the inside, she has been idle at Philadelphia since 1996 as preservationist groups continue to ponder over possibilities of saving her. One of the most recent was to see her as a moored hotel-casino at Philadelphia, Miami or New York. A continuing saga, the greatest American super liner has endured the greatest limbo.

After the first commercial jets crossed the Atlantic, beginning in October 1958, and all but immediately secured two-thirds of all clientele, ocean liners changed forever. By the 1960s, big liners had become big dinosaurs. But some saw hope in the future and this included the legendary French Line, which, in May 1960, launched a 66,000-ton, 2,000-passenger Atlantic liner. At 1,035ft in length, she was the longest liner yet and her distinctive profile was capped by two, winged funnels. Named *France*, she would be glamorous, lavish, her passengers exquisitely fed, but almost the last of a great breed. Initially designed to spend nine months in two-class Atlantic service and the other three in all one-class cruising, she offered superb public rooms, a large theatre, the finest food at sea and the last dog kennels to offer printed menus for pets. First-class travellers had the use of a prized facility: the celebrated Chambord Restaurant, perhaps the finest public room on a post-Second World War liner. Circular in shape

*▼ Vive la France!*
*The 66,348grt, 1,944-passenger* France *was the last of the great French liners when she was completed in 1962. (French Line)*

*The France was especially noted for her cooking: 'The finest French restaurant in the world,' proclaimed the* New York Times *in the 1960s. (Des Kirkpatrick Collection)*

and decorated in glass and aluminium, a large staircase descended into the space. She had a lavish collection of penthouses, suites and first-class cabins and a garage for passenger cars. There were even private servants' quarters. Tourist class included a considerable number of cabins with private bathroom facilities.

While she made several special cruises from New York to Rio de Janeiro for Carnival, the *France* also made, near the end of her French Line days in the early 1970s, two luxurious cruises around the world. These suited the ship's glamorous image. Some passengers took extra cabins just for their clothes, some flew in their favourite wines and some even brought along personal maids.

The *France* was supported, however, by a subsidy from the French Government,

but when that was discontinued in the fall of 1974 she was promptly withdrawn and laid up. Like many others, French Line passenger service ended abruptly. The

△ Moderne! The décor of the new, two-class *France* was very French contemporary. (French Line)

91

*Battle of the airlines! By the early 1970s, the* France *was losing too much money in the face of airline competition as well as drastically increased operating and fuel oil costs. At the age of twelve, in September 1974, she was withdrawn from service. (James Sesta Collection)*

*Transformation! In 1979–80, the indoor France was converted, at a West German shipyard, to the outdoor Norway. Now carrying a maximum of 2,565 passengers, she was then the largest cruise ship afloat. (Author's Collection)*

*▶ Thoughtful touches! The Norway carried two very large 400-capacity tenders to easily handle her passengers in otherwise smaller Caribbean ports. (Norwegian Cruise Lines)*

**Did you know?**
The first commercial flights by jet aircraft to cross the Atlantic in 1958 completely changed the future of Atlantic liner travel.

The Norway *sailed for another twenty-five years, cruising mostly in the Caribbean, but also to Europe (as seen here in Norway). (Author's Collection)*

**Did you know?**
There were 18,000 miles of wiring aboard the *France* of 1962.

impeccably reputed *France* had sailed for less than thirteen years. Some years later, in 1979–80, however, she found a new, very lucrative second career – as the largely rebuilt tropical cruise ship *Norway*, serving in the Caribbean from Miami on week-long cruises for the Norwegian Cruise Lines. She was the first large cruise ship, with some 2,200 beds in all, to sail year-round in leisure service. She continued until 2005, and then was scrapped in India four years later.

When she was completed in the spring of 1969, there were many critics that this $80 million ship would be a quick failure. After all, the jets had begun luring away Atlantic liner passengers for over a decade. The question was simple: who will fill what Cunard was calling 'the last Atlantic liner'? Yes, there were difficult early years, but the *Queen Elizabeth 2* developed a loyal and strong following.

◀ *End of an era! The* Queen Mary *sailed for thirty-one years and made over 1,000 crossings before she was retired from Cunard service in September 1967. (Des Kirkpatrick Collection)*

97

**Did you know?**
Said to be folly, the *Queen Elizabeth 2* sailed for thirty-nine years and became the most successful super liner of all time.

◄◄ *Farewell! When the* Queen Mary *left New York for the very last time, she was given a great, very sentimental farewell. (Author's Collection)*

◄ *The* Queen Elizabeth *left New York for the final time thirteen months later, in October 1968. (Author's Collection)*

*New lease of life! The Queen Mary avoided the scrappers and instead found further life as a moored museum, hotel and collection of shops and restaurants at Long Beach, California. (Hotel Queen Mary)*

*After forty years in southern California, the Queen Mary has endured – a lasting reminder of the great age of the ocean liner. (Hotel Queen Mary)*

Cleverly, by the 1980s, Cunard linked her five-night crossings with British Airways, including a luxury package that included a one-way crossing on Concorde. By the time she was retired in the fall of 2008 (and sold to buyers in Dubai for a staggering

◄ *Sad ending! On the eve of her maiden voyage in January 1972, the* Seawise University, *the former* Queen Elizabeth, *caught fire and burned out in Hong Kong harbour. She soon capsized and is seen here in this view two months later. (Des Kirkpatrick Collection)*

➤ *Renewal and rebirth! The* Queen Elizabeth 2, *the affectionately dubbed* QE2, *was said to be the rebirth of not only Atlantic liner travel, but of ocean voyaging in general when she was commissioned in May 1969. (Author's Collection)*

$100 million), she had been a huge success. She had the greatest records of any big liner in history. She had steamed more miles, visited more ports, carried more passengers and sailed for a record thirty-nine years. She also earned the most money. Yes, she was a great investment.

When the original *Queen Mary* (and later the *Queen Elizabeth* as well) was aging and due for replacement in the early 1960s, Cunard first looked to a traditional three-class ship as a replacement. But plans soon changed: to a two-class ship and one that spent half the year in Atlantic crossings, the other in one-class cruising. Cunard also wanted a new image. The ship might have been called British Queen, Britannia, Princess Anne, William Shakespeare, even Winston Churchill. But *Queen Elizabeth 2*, soon abbreviated to *QE2*, was the choice in

the end. Her Majesty the Queen named the ship, in September 1967, and at the same berth at the John Brown Shipyard on the Clyde where the earlier two Queens had been named and launched. Some traditions continued.

After numerous refits (including a conversion from steam to diesel in 1986/7)

*New style! Inside, the passenger quarters of the 2,005-passenger* QE2 *– with shopping malls, health spa and disco – seemed 'light years' away from the traditional ocean liner décor and styling. (Author's Collection)*

➤ *In 1982, following war duties in the South Atlantic during the Falklands War, the 963ft-long QE2 was briefly repainted with a light grey hull. (Author's Collection)*

➤➤ *In 1986–87, the QE2 became the last steamship on the Atlantic when she was converted to diesel propulsion in a massive transformation in a West German shipyard. (Cunard Line)*

and in her final years, the *QE2* took on great reverence and sentimentality. She was even seen as the 'last of the classic Atlantic liners'. Her voyages were often filled with loyalists to the great age of the liners. She might have gone to the scrappers in the very end, but Dubai buyers had other ideas. Their plan to make her over as a hotel, luxury residence, museum and collection of shops was put on hold as the worldwide recession set in by 2009. At the time of writing, the legendary *QE2*, no longer British and now registered at Port Vila, Vanuatu, waits at Port Rashid in Dubai for better economic times.

Once the *QE2* was to be retired, it was widely believed that even seasonal, half-year seasonal transatlantic liner service would end. Cunard had at times been considering a replacement, so it was rumoured, but did not have the financial means in the 1990s. Carnival Corporation came the rescue, in 1998, by purchasing the historic shipping company for $600 million and investing a further $800 million to build the 151,000-ton *Queen Mary 2*, the largest, longest, tallest and, in some ways, most lavish Atlantic liner of all time. She was commissioned, following a gala naming by Her Majesty the Queen at Southampton, in January 2004. She has been a great success ever since and has taken on the beloved role occupied by her predecessor, the *QE2*.

By 2010, with the addition of the 90,000-ton *Queen Victoria* and 92,000-ton *Queen Elizabeth*, Cunard had three liners and the newest fleet on the oceans. The *Queen Mary 2* is, of course, the flagship and is every inch the modern-day liner. She has shopping arcades, a planetarium, a grand ballroom, the largest library at sea,

▼ *A new Queen! After Cunard was bought by the Miami-based Carnival Corporation in 1998, monies were allocated to build the $800 million, 151,000-ton* Queen Mary 2. *(Cunard Line)*

▶ *Following her grandmother and her mother, Her Majesty Queen Elizabeth II named another Cunard Queen, the* Queen Mary 2, *in gala ceremonies at Southampton in January 2004. (Der Scutt Collection)*

▶▶ *Inaugural voyage: the 2,600-passenger* Queen Mary 2 *made a mid-Atlantic crossing, from Southampton to the Canaries, Madeira, the Caribbean and Florida, as her maiden voyage. (Der Scutt Collection)*

a Canyon Ranch health spa, grill rooms, a speciality restaurant and a luxurious, two-deck-high main dining room. Her top accommodations are duplex suites.

Between April and October, the 2,600-passenger *Queen Mary 2* runs regular seven-day crossings between New York and Southampton (with occasional extensions to Hamburg to tap into the lucrative German market); the remainder

◀ *Maritime grandeur! The splendid Britannia Dining Room aboard the* Queen Mary 2 *is reminiscent of the great age of the ocean liner. (Der Scutt Collection)*

*Hotel-like! The main lobby of the 1,132ft-long* Queen Mary 2, *the largest and longest Atlantic 'ocean liner' ever built, has the feel of a great hotel, a moving hotel. (Der Scutt Collection)*

*First meeting! In April 2004, the* Queen Mary 2 *met the then thirty-five-year-old* Queen Elizabeth 2 *at New York. (Maurizio Eliseo Collection)*

of the year is spent in cruising – from the likes of five-night voyages from New York to Halifax and Boston to 100 days around the world. In all, she has visited ports around the world and has become the most famous ocean liner afloat. She carries on the great traditions of the Cunard Line and is also the grand link to all of the super liners mentioned in these pages.

**Did you know?**
Her Majesty Queen Elizabeth II has named three great Cunard liners: the *Queen Elizabeth 2*, *Queen Mary 2* and *Queen Elizabeth.*

New York, 25th April 2004
The **QM2** and the **QE2**
*(Photography by Maurizio Eliseo)*

*Since the 1970s especially, cruising has boomed. In North America, over 6 million holidaymakers take cruises each year. (Royal Caribbean Cruise Lines)*

In 1980, the 70,000-ton *Queen Elizabeth 2* was said to be the last big liner ever to be built. When that thirty-nine-year-old ship was retired from active service in 2008, she was the eighty-ninth-largest passenger ship afloat. Liners grew in size dramatically,

◀◀◀ Floating resorts! More and more, and as liners have grown larger and larger, their accommodations and varied amenities make them seem like 'floating hotels', indeed resorts gone to sea. (Royal Caribbean Cruise Lines)

◀◀ Liner interiors today must include a 'wow factor', a design element that impresses passengers, especially first-timers. (Royal Caribbean Cruise Lines)

◀ Entrance lobbies, now rising to ten or twelve decks, are often the most impressive elements in modern-day cruise ship design. (Carnival Cruise Lines)

beginning in 1995, and continued at such a brisk pace that 100,000-ton liners carrying 3–4,000 passengers seemed almost ordinary. In just over a hundred years, we have gone from the 14,000-ton *Kaiser Wilhelm der Grosse* to the 225,000-ton *Allure of the Seas*.

Miami-based Royal Caribbean International, the world's second-largest cruise line, added no fewer than five sisters of the 142,000-ton, 3,400-passenger *Voyager of the Seas* class beginning in 1999. They were succeeded by the 160,000-ton, 4,200-berth *Freedom of the Seas* class in 2006 and finally, largest of all to date, the two sisters, *Oasis of the Seas* and *Allure of the Seas*, commissioned in 2009–10 and weighing in at 225,000 tons and carrying up to 6,400 travellers each. In between, in 2004, the historic Cunard Line, owned by another Miami-headquartered firm, the giant Carnival Corporation, since 1998, added the 151,000-ton *Queen Mary 2*. Carrying up to 2,600 passengers on half-year service between New York and Southampton, she is the largest, longest and tallest Atlantic liner ever.

By 2010, the greatest number of passengers of all time took to the seas. While destinations were often the sun-drenched Caribbean, Mediterranean, Latin American and South Pacific ports, there were also numerous trips to the likes of Alaska, Scandinavia, the very top of Norway and even remote Arctic waters. There were cruise offerings from remote ports as well – such as Dubai, the Seychelles or Ushuaia in southern Argentina. Ports of call ranged from Fort Lauderdale to the Falkland Islands, from Seattle to Sydney,

**Did you know?**
The 101,000-ton *Carnival Destiny*, commissioned in 1996, was the first liner to exceed 100,000 gross tons.

from Shanghai to Samoa. Alone, eleven million took to the seas in the United States and, adding to this, the likes of 1.5 million departed from British ports, nearly a million from Germany and 500,000 from Spain. Cruising, on amenity-filled,

**Did you know?**
The *Voyager of the Seas*, completed in 1999, was the first liner to have a complete ice-skating arena on board.

◀ *Carnival Corporation is today the largest passenger shipowner and operator, with some 100 liners belonging to fourteen cruise line subsidiaries. (Carnival Cruise Lines)*

creature-comfortable floating resorts, is increasingly seen as excellent holiday value. Yet, in the United States, only 15 per cent of all holidaymakers have taken their first cruise. Cruise lines project an increase, perhaps even to 20 per cent, which means

**Did you know?**
The 225,000-ton sisters *Oasis of the Seas* and *Allure of the Seas*, the largest liners ever built, have a recreated version of Central Park in New York City as a design highlight.

another 5 million annual voyagers. Clearly, further significant growth in the cruise industry is ahead.

Cruising, which began in the 1840s aboard smallish P&O steamers on voyages 'of educational and scientific discovery,' was the domain of the rich and the select until the 1920s. The general public took to them more by the 1930s, years of the sinister Depression, but as inexpensive methods of escapism. The Nazi party in Germany built the world's very first large cruise ship in 1938, the 2,000-passenger *Wilhelm Gustloff*, which was used for workers' propaganda voyages. General cruising greatly resumed and in earnest in the 1970s and produced the first generations of purpose-built cruise ships. Growth was steady, very successful and well beyond expectation. By 1996, Carnival Cruise Lines, the biggest and most successful operator anywhere (they owned fourteen cruise lines and some 100 passenger ships by 2011), created the first liner to exceed the 100,000-ton mark, the 3,360-passenger *Carnival Destiny*. She might have been the end, but instead was the thirty-fifth-largest liner afloat by 2010. Liners well over 100,000 tons, more than 900ft in length and carrying up to 4,000 passengers seemed to be the norm. In 2008, forty-eight new cruise ships were either on order or under construction. It is doubtful, however, that any ship will exceed the 225,000 tons, 6,400-passenger capacity level of the *Allure of the Seas* and her twin sister. For their next class, Royal Caribbean is building slightly smaller ships, the 150,000-ton 'Project Sunshine' class. Carnival Cruise Lines' latest ship was the 130,000-ton *Carnival Magic* while

Princess Cruises had ordered (in 2010) twin sisters of 140,000 tons and P&O its largest liner ever, a 141,000-ton vessel with twin funnels.

Clearly, the story of *The Great Liners* will continue for many years to come!

**Did you know?**

In 2011, more holidaymakers were travelling by ship than ever before.

*▼ Among the projects on the drawing board in 2011 was a new, French-built version of the* France. *This new creation, intended to be 60,000 tons and carry 700 cruise passengers, is projected for completion in 2015.*

Le nouveau «France» marque l'avènement d'une nouvelle génération de paquebots de croisière : lignes innovantes, moindre consommation, plus d'espace et de confort pour ses passagers.

Embarquez à bord du FRANCE
Cap sur 2015

◀ *The* Queen Elizabeth 2 *arriving in Sydney, February 2007. (Author's Collection)*

▶ *The* Queen Mary 2 *arrives at San Francisco, January 2007. (Author's Collection)*

➤ *The 225,000gt* Allure of the Seas *(left) and the 142,000gt* Voyager of the Seas *at Labadee, Haiti, in January 2011. (Author's Collection)*

◀ *The* Allure of the Seas *alone at Labadee, Haiti, in January 2011. (Author's Collection)*

▲ *The* Queen Elizabeth *at New York, September 2011. (Author's Collection)*

Braynard, Frank O. and Miller, William H., *Fifty Famous Liners, Vols 1–3*. Cambridge, England: Patrick Stephens Ltd, 1982–86

Devol, George and Cassidy, Thomas (eds), *Ocean and Cruise News*. Stamford, Connecticut: World Ocean and Cruise Liner Society, 1980–2010

Mayes, William, *Cruise Ships* (revised edition). Windsor: Overview Press Ltd, 2009

Miller, William H., *British Ocean Liners: A Twilight Era 1960–85*. New York: W.W. Norton & Co., 1986

--- *Great British Passenger Ships*. Stroud, Gloucestershire: The History Press, 2010

--- *Floating Palaces: The Great Atlantic Liners*. Stroud, Gloucestershire: Amberley Publishing, 2011

--- *Pictorial Encyclopedia of Ocean Liners 1864–1994*. Mineola, New York: Dover Publications Inc., 1995

--- *Picture History of British Ocean Liners*. Mineola, New York: Dover Publications Inc., 2001

--- *Picture History of the Cunard Line 1840–1990*. Mineola, New York: Dover Publications Inc., 1991

THE **HMS VICTORY** STORY

■ ISBN 978 0 7524 5605 8

THE **QE2** STORY

■ ISBN 978 0 7524 5094 0

THE **CUNARD** STORY

■ ISBN 978 0 7524 5914 1

THE **QM2** STORY

■ ISBN 978 0 7524 5092 6

THE **HOVERCRAFT** STORY

■ ISBN 978 0 7524 6128 1

THE **MARY ROSE** STORY

■ ISBN 978 0 7524 6404 6